Under

Attack

How The Tea Party

Can Fight Back And Win!

Larry Nichols

The Political Guru Who Uncovered The
Scandals That Led To The Impeachment
Of President Bill Clinton

Table of Contents

Introduction

Those of us who are 50 years of age and older have seen changes in our lives that are major and frequent. Every day we have seen a greater loss of liberty, and we are repeatedly forced to endure more intrusions into our personal lives.

This handbook is designed to let you know that you are not alone in recognizing the numerous violations of our personal liberty by those in positions of power. Also, it is my sincere desire to arm you with some simple tools that you must use and share with others. By understanding and employing these simple tools, together, we can stop and reverse the systematic destruction of our country from within – before it is too late!

As we cover what is happening in Washington, D.C. today, I will explain how both major parties have declared open warfare against the Tea Party, including warfare against the remnants of Jerry Falwell's Moral Majority. The leaders of both major parties understand that it was Jerry Falwell's morally-based group of committed conservative Christians that successfully challenged the liberal movement of that day and swept Ronald Reagan into office. And, it was the Reagan Revolution of the 1980s that gave us hope that we could stop and reverse the liberal shift that had taken place within the federal government.

Today, that level of hope no longer exists. Today, true conservatives are lost! We have seen how the leadership of the Republican Party in Washington has abandoned the ideals of the Reagan Revolution and has merged with the leftist leadership of the Democratic Party. Together, they control most of the political agenda in Washington, D.C. Collectively, they are waging open warfare against the Tea Party and the remnants of the Moral Majority!

Presently, those of you in the Tea Party find yourselves virtually alone in pursuit of your goals! You recognize that you are receiving no real support from the leadership of the Republican Party at the federal level. Instead of finding support from a political party that traditionally claimed to be of like mind, you now find that the Republican leadership has publicly announced their intent to "crush" you and your fellow

Tea Party members – which have historically been valued as a vital and significant part of the conservative base of the Republican Party.

I recognize and thoroughly understand the plight facing you and your fellow Tea Party warriors as well as that of all moral conservative Christian soldiers. I understand your loss of hope and sense of frustration with those in power within the Republican Party, for I was in a similar position back in the 1990s when the personal war between Bill Clinton and I began. At that point I found myself aligned with the Christian Moral Majority as well as those pioneering conservative talk radio.

Then, as now, I was disappointed to learn that, at almost every turn the Republican leadership was uninterested in supporting my efforts to combat the Democratic Party's leftist political machinery. After repeated frustration with their lack of support, I concluded that, in effect, we the people were being governed by only one party, and the two party system was merely a mirage.

So, embrace the ideas outlined in this handbook, and use the tools that were developed to pave the way for the impeachment of the most powerful person in the world at that time – Bill Clinton, President of the United States! I intend to do my part to save my country. Also, I will do everything in my power to reinstate God in his rightful place in our government. And to accomplish this I need an army, and you are it! As you finish this Introduction and begin reading Chapter One, keep in mind the following quote:

"I call on every officer and man...to live and act as becomes a Christian soldier, defending the dearest rights and liberties of his country." – George Washington, 1st President of the United States, and "Father of Our Nation."

Chapter One

What Is Actually Happening

With Washington!

How It Has Changed And Why!

For years in the political world it was believed that, in order to get elected, candidates must offend the least number of people. It was not how many people you pleased, but instead, victory went to the least offensive candidate. However, a new political tactic was used by the Clinton's in Arkansas, and it has now permeated Washington, D.C.

This new political tactic is known as polarization. Under polarization the candidate selects a group to become a political target. The politically targeted group is repeatedly attacked to engender anger among the group members. However, unknown to the uninitiated, the primary purpose of the attack is not to anger the target, but to secure the support of the target's political enemies. In brief, the candidate attacks the target so the enemies of the target become the allies and political supporters of the candidate.

So, the tactic of offending the least number of people has been replaced with the tactic of deliberately offending a strategically targeted group of individuals. Consequently, the target group and their political opponents become polarized, thus justifying the term "polarization."

I have learned over the years that, you can uncover the agenda of a given politician or political group simply by observing patterns in their behavior. Their behavioral patterns offer clues to their final goal. However, what is confusing, at least on its surface, is the pattern of behavior by the Republican establishment to "crush" the Tea Party and the moral Christian majority that has been a consistently loyal constituency.

Those who follow politics have observed this baffling phenomenon within the leadership of the Republican Party. Two prominent Republicans, U.S. Senator Mitch McConnell of Kentucky, and former U.S. Representative

Steve LaTourette of Ohio, have openly declared their intent to raise millions of dollars for the sole purpose of destroying the Tea Party.

However, members of the Tea Party have been an integral part of the Republican base, and it was instrumental in giving the Republicans control of the U.S. House of Representatives in the 2010 mid-term elections. In addition, it is a powerful political force that could also help Republicans gain control of the U.S. Senate in the 2014 mid-term elections as well.

So, how do we explain a pattern of behavior by the Republican leadership that is clearly detrimental to the Republican Party and obviously beneficial to the Democratic Party? The explanation is as follows: There is something more important to the Republican leader-ship than the welfare of the Republican Party, and that "something" is personal political power! They are placing their personal political welfare far above the welfare of the Republican Party and above the welfare of the nation they claim to serve!

It is becoming clear that the hierarchy of the "Old Guard" of the Republican Party feels so threatened that they are willing to expose themselves as members of a political elite that is more closely aligned with the leadership of the Democratic Party than with the base of the Republican Party. They fear that the 2014 mid-term elections may usher in enough Tea Party candidates and Tea Party supported candidates that they may achieve enough power to literally redefine the Republican Party.

Adopting the tactic of political polarization employed by Democrat Bill Clinton, the Republican leadership has publicly targeted the Tea Party for destruction. By openly declaring war on the Tea Party, they have invited moderates and liberals from both major political parties to side with them in attacking and destroying Tea Party members and their supporters as well. Yes, the enemy of my enemy is my friend. It is a shrewd political move, but it exposed their true allegiance.

For many decades we have been led to believe that there are two major political parties in Washington, D.C., one liberal and one conservative. But in fact, behind the scenes, there is only one. Mitch McConnell, John McCain, John Boehner, and others, are in Washington for one purpose: to acquire and maintain personal political power – at the expense of the party and at the expense of the nation, if necessary. They show us the facade of two parties when necessary, but they also show us the reality of one party, when left with no choice!

This newly exposed allegiance among the elite of both major parties helps to explain a phenomenon that conservatives have complained about for many years. When establishment Republicans battle Democrats, they always seem to fight with one hand tied behind their backs. However, when they battle conservative Republicans, establishment Republicans fight with both hands – and with both feet!

If the current level of animosity directed toward the Tea Party had been directed toward Barack Obama prior to the 2008 presidential election, then Senator Obama would not be called President Obama today. If the Republican leadership had exposed Barack Obama's true, sordid, longstanding relationship with the likes of Bill Ayers and Bernardine Dohrn – who led the domestic Communist terrorist organization known as the Weather Underground, today we would be living in a very different America. There would be no ObamaCare train wreck and cover-up; no deadly Fast & Furious scandal and cover-up; no fatal Benghazi scandal and cover-up; no IRS scandal and cover-up; no White House-directed immigration reform, and no repeated embarrassments on the international scene!

Yes, the elite Republicans who want Ted Cruz out of the U.S. Senate, are the same elite Republicans who helped Barack Obama plant his feet on top of the desk in the Oval Office! The elite of both parties are on the same team, thus, in reality, there is only one party! This is what is happening in Washington, D.C. today. This is how it has changed, and why it has changed. In effect, we the people are now governed by a single band of elitists in pursuit of absolute, unchallengeable power.

For the first time in our history, our very form of government is changing right before our eyes. Democrat Barack Obama is not the only politician in Washington who wants to fundamentally transform America. Often-times, he is doing it with the help of the Republican leadership! Why has the leadership of the Republican Party allowed Obama to repeatedly bypass Congress and legislate from the Oval Office?

If the Republican Party was truly an opposition party, there would be real opposition to Obama's repeated lawlessness in sidestepping Congress. Instead of opposition, the Republican leadership routinely offers false hope to voters who want to see a genuine return to honest, lawful, constitutional government at the federal level.

Sadly, President Abraham Lincoln's government of the people, by the people, and for the people, has been essentially malformed into government of the elite, by the elite, and for the elite! Time is short. The Tea Party must not only survive this onslaught wrought by the Republican leadership and its Democrat allies, it must rise up and outsmart, outmaneuver, and defeat this elitist group in 2014, 2016, and beyond. And that, my fellow patriots, it the purpose of this handbook!

Chapter Two

The United States Congress!

What Value Does It Actually Have Today?

Who Changed Its Role As A Co-Equal Branch

Of Government?

When our forefathers set up our form of government, they created three separate, co-equal branches. It was set up in this manner to construct a system of checks and balances. This three-part governmental system was designed to prevent the concentration of power in a single individual or a single group.

Our forefathers lived under the despotism of King George III of Great Britain. Because they personally experienced the tyranny of concentrated governmental power, they concluded that a divided form of government was essential for establishing and maintaining a nation where individual liberty could flourish. When they created our government, they did not necessarily know what form of government was unquestionably right, but they most definitely knew what form of government was unquestionably wrong!

Obama and others have complained about a "do nothing" Congress, or an "obstructionist" Congress. But there are times when we want a "do nothing" Congress. We want a "do nothing" Congress when it is best to do nothing than to pass unconstitutional legislation that diminishes personal liberty. But we don't want a "do nothing" Congress when the president or the U.S. Supreme Court oversteps their constitutional authority. When the clearly defined separation of powers is violated, then we want an "obstructionist" Congress. We want Congress to obstruct all efforts by the president or the U.S. Supreme Court to exceed their constitutional limitations and encroach upon the powers and authority granted only to the U.S. Congress.

Obama complains about a "do nothing" Congress, for example, regarding immigration reform. He has told us emphatically that he has a pen and a phone, and he will use these tools to fundamentally transform America – without the benefit of legislation passed by Congress –

if he deems it necessary to advance his agenda. The U.S. Constitution states that all legislative power rests with the U.S. Congress. The U.S. Supreme Court lacks the legal authority to legislate from the bench, and the U.S. President has absolutely no legal authority to legislate from the Oval Office. However, Obama has altered his signature piece of legislation, the so-called Affordable Care Act, better known as ObamaCare, several dozen times. Each of these changes was made in blatant violation of the U.S. Constitution's clearly defined separation of powers. Only the U.S. Congress has the constitutional authority to create or alter legislation, including ObamaCare!

For decades the legislative branch has allowed the judicial branch to legislate from the bench, thus robbing Congress of its constitutionally delegated powers. Now, with Barack Obama following in the footsteps of the U.S. Supreme Court, Congress is allowing itself to be placed on a dangerous path. With the development of an imperial presidency, the U.S. Congress may soon find itself demoted to a mere ceremonial role, perhaps something akin to that found in Czarist Russia or the old Soviet Union.

Now more than ever, the constitutional roles of the three branches of government have been blurred, and the executive branch is being catapulted into a position of near unlimited power, the scope of which is seen only in dictatorships! We must return to our roots. We the people must return to the wisdom of our forefathers and demand that each of the three branches of the federal government operate within the limitations placed upon them by the U.S. Constitution.

However, this goal can only be achieved when we the people elect representatives who respect the U.S. Constitution and the rule of law. We can only achieve this goal by removing the current leaders of the Republican Party now running the U.S. Congress, and replacing them with Tea Party members and those who are aligned with the Tea Party. That must be our goal, and that goal must be achieved. Failure is not an option. The stakes are much too high! As you soldier on, keep in mind these quotes from our Founding Fathers:

"...in questions of power then, let no more be heard of confidence in man, but bind him down from mischief by the chains of the constitution..." – Thomas Jefferson, 3rd President of the United States of America

Thus, Thomas Jefferson tried to warn future generations that politicians cannot be trusted. Therefore, we
must confine them to the limits placed upon them by
the Constitution, or they may become no different than
common criminals and rob us of everything we cherish.

John Adams, 2nd U.S. President, stated the following:
"Posterity! You will never know how much it cost the
present Generation to preserve your Freedom! I hope
you will make good use of it." Clearly, the freedom we
Americans have traditionally enjoyed was earned by the
blood, sweat, and tears of our forefathers and everyone
who followed them in fighting to preserve our
constitutional republic and our national sovereignty.
Have we made good use of that hard fought freedom,
or have we allowed ourselves to be deceived into
surrendering our liberty in exchange for a false sense of
security? As Benjamin Franklin correctly stated, "Those
who would give up essential Liberty, to purchase a little
temporary Safety, deserve neither Liberty nor Safety."

"But a Constitution of Government once changed
from Freedom, can never be restored. Liberty, once lost,
is lost forever." – John Adams, 2nd President of the
United States of America

John Adams was correct. History teaches us that once liberty is lost, it is never fully recovered. We are truly at a crossroads in America today. We can either continue to surrender our liberty for false security, or we can follow in the footsteps of our forefathers. We can either fight for liberty, or surrender to tyranny! The real question is this: Do we have the boldness of Patrick Henry, a courageous Founding Father who boldly stated, "Give me liberty, or give me death?"

Chapter Three

Does The United States Of America Still Exist, And Do The American People Still Have Any Rights?

In writing this chapter, I am forced to reflect upon some vital questions, and would suggest that everyone who reads this handbook, do the same. We are at a point in time when we must ask, can we still call ourselves Americans today? Do we have any rights that cannot be violated by Washington politicians, bureaucrats, and judicial activists?

I fear that we the people have lost most, if not all, of our connection to our forefathers. Over many generations we have lost sight of our solemn duty to remain vigilant and closely monitor our government leaders.

When asking the question, do the American people still exist, I must answer, I don't know! This answer may seem to be a copout, but it is not. Ask yourself, do you really believe that the American revolutionaries of 1776 that we read about in our history books, would recognize us as their "fellow Americans?" Do we have the same spirit of independence as those early Americans who wrote the Declaration of Independence and the U.S. Constitution? Do we have the same courage as those American patriots who risked their lives to defeat the British Army and Navy, which comprised the world's most powerful military at that point in time?

After fighting a brutal war for independence from governmental control, how would our forefathers describe the tens of millions of contemporary Americans who eagerly surrendered their hard-fought independence and replaced it with total or near total dependence upon government? How would they view the Americans today who have voluntarily surrendered their economic liberty in order to receive minimal economic security in the form of monthly checks and food stamps? Would they even recognize us as fellow Americans?

As noted in the previous chapter, our forefather, Patrick Henry, courageously stated, "Give me liberty, or give me death!" How many Americans would still say that today? How many Americans would now say, "Don't give me liberty, give me dependency!" "Don't give me liberty, give me a government check!" Clearly, many of us have severed our psychological ties with the independent-minded revolutionaries who founded this great nation!

Every check issued by the federal government expands its size and scope. By supplying tens of millions of taxpayer-funded checks on a monthly basis, it extends its reach into every important area of our lives, from health care, to education, retirement, communication, and transportation, to name just a few.

Most importantly, such learned dependence fosters a compliant and submissive attitude which paves the way for massive governmental intrusions into our personal, daily lives. Soon we find ourselves living under the so-called "Patriot Act," and the FBI, CIA, NSA, and other government snoops monitor our emails, telephone calls, and banking transactions. With Medicare, Medicaid, and ObamaCare, the federal government monitors, and even determines, our personal health care choices. They even enter our homes without a warrant. All of this intrusive governmental behavior has rendered our Fourth Amendment rights null and void!

Clearly, the 9/11 terrorists attacks destroyed more than the Twin Towers and the two passenger airliners that brought them down. It did more than damage the Pentagon and obliterate the passenger airliner that penetrated deeply into its interior. Finally, it did more than bring down and demolish a passenger airliner in a Pennsylvania field!

In addition to all this damage, the 9/11 terrorist attacks destroyed the will of far too many Americans to resist intrusive government! At that point, an increasing number of Americans cut their ties with our forefathers. Many of us simply stopped being freedom-loving Americans! Far too many people willingly surrendered liberty for a false sense of security. As noted in the previous chapter, our forefather, Benjamin Franklin, correctly stated that, "Those who would give up essential Liberty, to purchase a little temporary Safety, deserve neither Liberty nor Safety."

Unknown to many Americans, by surrendering our liberty in exchange for government-imposed security, the terrorists have won! Their goal is to destroy America, and by destroying traditional American liberty they have most certainly destroyed America. Indeed, for many in this nation the terrorists have truly demolished the independent American spirit that guided George Washington, Thomas Jefferson, James Madison, and many more of our Founding Fathers. With massive government-imposed security we now have a growing police state; therefore, we can no longer say we are "the land of the free and the home of the brave!"

But not all Americans are willing to surrender their personal liberty in exchange for a false sense of security imposed by unrestrained politicians and government bureaucrats. And it is within this group of freedom-loving Americans that we find members of the Tea Party, as well as those who describe themselves as Christian conservatives, constitutional conservatives, fiscal conservatives, social conservatives, and even self-described libertarians!

Yes, it is through the joining of like minds among grassroots, liberty-loving individuals that offers any true hope of restoration. Only among those who continue to think like traditional Americans and act like traditional

Americans will we find the mindset necessary to re-establish the America founded by our forefathers!

Our forefathers overcame seemingly insurmountable obstacles to create the United States of America. The challenges they faced far exceed the challenges we face today. This is not an underestimation of the trials and tribulations we face, but rather a recognition of the fact that, if they could overcome their monumental barriers to victory, we most certainly can overcome ours.

So, does the United States of America still exist? Remember, the United States of America is, above all else, an idea! Therefore, it most certainly does not exist in the minds of establishment Republicans and elitist Democrats who are now running Washington, D.C. And, it no longer exists in the minds of those in the leftist media and education establishment. However, America is alive and well in the minds of Tea Party members and all those who are aligned with this movement!

Therefore, if members from these groups can replace the current leadership in Washington, D.C., the America of our forefathers, along with the rights enshrined in the U.S. Constitution, can most certainly be restored! If, like

Patrick Henry, enough Americans emphatically state, "Give me liberty, or give me death," we cannot, and we will not, fail!

Chapter Four

Why The Pledge Of Allegiance

Is A Lie Today!

This chapter was inspired by a good friend who recently attended a meeting of fellow patriots. At the onset of this meeting everyone rose to recite the Pledge of Allegiance, which has been a common practice among loyal Americans for many generations. However, as the group began to speak, my friend realized she could no longer recite the words, although she had cherished this historic pledge from early childhood.

She could not join this group of fellow patriots because, as she began to utter these solemn words, she realized they were no longer true! She was struck by the undeniable fact that the Pledge of Allegiance today, is in fact, a lie! When she conveyed this observation to me, I concluded that she had made a very profound statement, and it served as a clear indicator of the real state of our union today.

When listening to the crowd reciting the words of the Pledge of Allegiance, she realized the extent to which our nation has been fundamentally transformed from within. So, she stood silently as they recited the following words: "I pledge allegiance to the Flag of the United States of America, and to the Republic for which it stands, one nation under God, indivisible, with liberty and justice for all."

It almost sounds sacrilegious when I say the Pledge of Allegiance is a lie! We certainly do not want this historic pledge to be riddled with falsehoods. But let's dissect it line by line. Firstly we say, "I pledge allegiance to the Flag of the United States of America." This line certainly remains true today, assuming the person who utters these words truly pledges his or her allegiance to our flag.

Next we say, "And to the Republic for which it stands." Now, search your memory, and try to recall any politician, at any level of government, who has referred to our nation as a "Republic." Instead, they always seem to refer to America as a "Democracy." Our forefathers were very clear on this issue. In Article IV, Section 4 of the U.S. Constitution, we find the following statement:

"The United States shall guarantee to every state in this Union, a republican form of government,..." Also, in the second paragraph of Article VI it is stated that the U.S. Constitution "Shall be the supreme law of the land." The U.S. Constitution guarantees each state a republican form of government, and the U.S. Constitution is unquestionably the supreme law of the land. It is for these reasons that our Pledge of Allegiance states, "And to the Republic for which it stands." This is precisely why it does not say, "And to the Democracy for which it stands."

Why did our forefathers create a republic and not a democracy? And, why are politicians, bureaucrats, media personnel, and educators, trying to deceive us into believing we are a democracy – when the word democracy cannot be found anywhere in the U.S. Constitution?

In a republican form of government the supreme power is held by the citizens who vote, and that power is exercised through their elected politicians – who are to govern according to the law of the land. In a democracy the supreme power is also held by the people who vote, however, that power is exercised by majority rule, not by elected politicians who are restrained by the rule of law. So, a democracy allows for unlimited power under majority rule, and the majority may do whatever it wishes to do. Individuals within a minority group may become subservient to the majority, and the minority may have few, if any rights. For this reason our forefathers wisely created a republic wherein the majority is restrained by law, and they vigorously denounced democracy as an illegitimate form of government.

For example, Thomas Jefferson stated that "a democracy is nothing more than mob rule, where fifty-one percent of the people may take away the rights of the other forty-nine." In addition, Benjamin Franklin stated that "Democracy is two wolves and a lamb voting on what to have for lunch. Liberty is a well-armed lamb contesting the vote!" Thus, a republic is far superior to a democracy because it protects the natural right of the minority to be unmolested by the majority.

With these definitions in mind, we can see why elite politicians of both major parties refer to our nation as a democracy instead of a republic. Through the media and education establishment they can incite a mob rule mentality among the majority of voters. For example, they can instigate class warfare against the "rich" and force them to pay their "fair share" to the non-rich, regardless of what the law may say. Also, the majority may codify laws to permit what Walter E. Williams calls "legalized theft" of our hard-earned money. And the money confiscated through a mob rule democracy is always used to build a massive, powerful government, and to buy the votes of the majority to keep power-hungry politicians in power! Sadly, this is precisely what we have in Washington, D.C. today, and this is why my friend and I have concluded that the Pledge of Allegiance has become, regrettably, a bold faced lie!

Lastly, in the Pledge of Allegiance we find these words: "One nation under God, indivisible, with liberty and justice for all." However, we may ask, are we "one nation under God," or one nation under mob rule? Are we "indivisible," or are we divided by those inciting class warfare between the poor and the rich; warfare by non-whites against whites; warfare by Islamists, atheists, and agnostics against Bible-believing Christians; warfare by global warming supporters against global warming skeptics, etc. etc. etc? Clearly, we have been divided in more ways than can be listed in this handbook! America, the so-called "melting pot," is gone!

Abraham Lincoln, referring to a passage in the Bible (*Mark 3:25*), correctly stated that, a house divided against itself cannot stand. Therefore, when politicians, media pundits, and educators divide us, we are no longer a nation of "We the people," but rather a nation where we have an "us against them" mentality! Yes, on many important issues, we have become polarized.

Do we enjoy "liberty and justice for all" today, or do we now have liberty and justice for some? It was recently announced that author and TV pitchman Kevin Trudeau has been sentenced to 10 years in prison for misleading advertising, selling a faulty product, and repeatedly ignoring the law. However, how much time will Obama serve for deliberately misleading us about ObamaCare, selling us this faulty product, and repeatedly ignoring the supreme law of the land by bypassing Congress and altering ObamaCare from the Oval Office? Yes, we now have liberty and justice for some, but not for all!

Sadly, today we must now say, "I pledge allegiance to the Flag, and to the Democracy for which it stands, one nation under mob rule, divisible, with liberty and justice for some." Notice that this Pledge of Allegiance says, "I pledge allegiance to the Flag," but it does not say "of the United States of America." These words are absent because the nation described in this pledge does not remotely resemble the nation depicted in the U.S. Constitution. It is not the nation founded by George Washington, Thomas Jefferson, and James Madison. However, it does accurately describe the nation in which we now live. And this is precisely why the authentic Pledge of Allegiance is a lie today!

Chapter Five

What Is The Tea Party?

How Can It Survive Now That Both National

Parties Have Sworn To Destroy It?

There are two distinct concepts that define the Tea Party today. The first concept is that of an organic grassroots group of patriotic individuals who believe in limited government. They believe the current federal government should be reduced in its size and scope. These are the fiscally responsible Americans who are truly concerned about excessive spending and the frightening increase in our national debt. They are also concerned about the multiple, massive federal bureaucracies that have been built as a result of this reckless spending and debt.

Equally troubling is our government's quest to remove God from government property and seemingly from our way of life. Among those who maintain strong Christian beliefs, these governmental actions create a significant level of fear. Many fear that the removal of God from our nation may have grave consequences.

The Bible is full of warnings of what happens to nations when their people turn away from God. Our Founding Fathers were committed to keeping our nation under the blessings and protection of God. As Bible believing Christians, they knew that when nations turned their backs on God, the blessings and protection of God were removed and they suffered total annihilation. They did not want to see their creation destroyed in this manner.

The second conceptualization of the Tea Party is held by powerful individuals who now control our central government. They are the politicians who occupy the leadership of both major political parties! These power-hungry career politicians see the Tea Party as a "game changer" that must be stopped at any cost. In their eyes, the Tea Party represents a dire threat to the centralized governmental power many have spent a lifetime to attain. To them, the Tea Party has the potential to return a significant amount of power back to the states and to the people, as envisioned by our

Founding Fathers. They fear we may once again become a nation of laws, and not a nation of men.

The Tea Party is unique! Unlike other national parties and national organizations, it does not have a single top leader to act as overseer or chief executive officer. Instead, it is made up of numerous small groups spread all across this great country. Therefore, the Tea Party has many leaders – and no master. Although the Tea Party is made up of numerous separate groups, they are united in their desire to reduce the size of government and protect our liberty.

Lacking a single master or overseer, the Tea Party is not easily penetrated and subverted by its political enemies. No doubt, if the Tea Party had the same formal status and hierarchical structure as found in the two major national parties, sooner or later it would be infiltrated and subverted by the political enemies who desperately seek to destroy it. As a consequence, we would have three major national parties with corrupt leadership instead of just two major national parties with corrupt leadership.

When Bill Clinton became President of the United States and assumed the leadership of the Democratic

Party, he brought with him a staunch liberal mindset. Although he was a practical politician who was willing to work toward comprise to pass legislation, he had a decided leftist bent. For this reason some of the "Old Guard" conservative Democrats felt compelled to become Republicans, stating, like Ronald Reagan before them, that they did not leave the Democratic Party, but rather the Democratic Party left them! So, we still had the same people, but just in a different party. As a consequence of a transfer of Democrats over a period of many years, the Republican Party became much less conservative and it has lost its way. This shift away from conservatism within the Republican Party is what spawned the Tea Party movement.

As you will read repeatedly throughout this hand-book, the two major national political parties have become, in effect, just one party. They play against one another seeking positions of power, but all too often they do not play against one another to advance opposing agendas. True conservatives within the Republican Party have recognized this unholy alliance among the elites of both major political parties, and they have taken action to counteract it. They formed the Tea Party movement!

I want you to know what the Republican establishment knows and what I know: If there is a massive turnout of Tea Party members and other grassroots conservative Republicans in primary elections, you can most certainly defeat the Mitch McConnell-supported and Steve LaTourette-supported candidates. You can take back the party. And you most certainly know that, before you can take back America, you must first take back the Republican Party!

The Republican leadership knows that about 50 percent of Republican primary voters nationwide will be Tea Party members and other grassroots conservatives. In addition, about 6 to 10 percent of the Republican primary voters nationwide will be hardcore, statist Republicans who consistently vote according to the desires of the Republican establishment. Finally, the Republican leadership knows that among Republican primary voters, about 40 percent will be moderates who can be persuaded to vote for the Tea Party candidate if given the proper message. However, they can also vote for the establishment Republican candidate if the only message they hear comes from the Republican leadership. Therefore, a powerful, persuasive Tea Party message is the key to victory!

The conservative 50 percent must persuade the moderate 40 percent to join with them. This can be accomplished by educating them about the fact that Mitch McConnell, Steve LaTourette, and other establishment Republicans seek to destroy the Tea Party and everything it stands for, including fiscal sanity!

Tea Party members, other conservatives, and every single moderate, must be told over and over again that when they vote for the Tea Party candidate in the primary election, they are not simply voting against a non-Tea Party opponent, they are truly voting against the Republican establishment that wants to destroy the Tea Party and the liberty the Tea Party represents. When they vote for the Tea Party member they are also voting against the representatives of Mitch McConnell, Steve LaTourette, and every other elitist Republican who is drunk on power and working to destroy our efforts to return to honest, lawful, constitutional government! This message must be conveyed not only by the Tea Party as a group, but, perhaps even more importantly, by every individual member of the Tea Party. Every individual member of the Tea Party must become a walking billboard, targeting every single conservative and moderate within reach.

Repeatedly drive home this vitally important point: Tea Party members are the true representatives of the grassroots Americans who have maintained a genuine, deep-seated psychological, philosophical, and political connection to our Founding Fathers. They are the true lovers of liberty who are following in the footsteps of George Washington, Thomas Jefferson, James Madison, and Patrick Henry. So, convince every conservative and every moderate in the party that they must work together, fight together, and pray together. If we do this, we will most certainly win together!

We are in a war. It is a political war, but it is none-the-less a war! We are fighting for the heart and soul of the Republican Party, and the heart and soul of America! Yes, the Republican establishment has declared war on the Tea Party. That means the Republican establishment, like the Democrat establishment, is at war with the founding principles that has made this nation the greatest nation on Earth! Surrender is not an option. If will lose this war – a war we did not start – our children and grandchildren will never know what it is truly like to live and breathe as a free American.

Look around you. Gaze upon that which is most important to you. Fix your attention upon the people you love more than life itself. You realize there is much in your life worth fighting for, and dying for! Yes, you would risk everything to protect that which you love. Transfer that feeling to love of country, and love of liberty! Yes, the America you love is worth fighting for. It is worth dying for!

I would like to close this chapter with a quote from Ronald Reagan, the 40th President of the United States of America. Take this handbook with you, and recite Reagan's words to everyone who will listen before they head to the polls to vote:

"Freedom is never more than one generation away from extinction. We didn't pass it to our children in the bloodstream. It must be fought for, protected, and handed down for them to do the same, or one day we will spend our sunset years telling our children and our children's children what it was once like in the United States when men were free."

Chapter Six

Immigration:

It's Not About Jobs;

It's About Cancelling Out Your Vote!

Immigration reform reportedly designed to fill jobs that Americans will not take is a deceptive cover story. Don't buy it. More than any other purpose, immigration is about votes!

According to the *U.S. Census Bureau*, there were about 317 million people living in America at the end of 2013. About 17 percent, or 54 million, are described as Hispanic or Latino. The foreign born from all races and ethnicities make up about 13 percent of the U.S. population. We know that illegal aliens operate within the shadows of society, so an unknown number are not counted by the *U.S. Census Bureau*.

Today, about 20 million of the 54 million Hispanics are eligible to vote. In the 2012 presidential election Hispanics made up about 10 percent of the electorate. To no one's surprise, in the 2012 presidential election Democrat Barack Obama received 71 percent of the Hispanic vote, and Republican Mitt Romney received only 27 percent. In election after election, Democrats consistently win a majority of Hispanic votes. Beyond all doubt, this is the primary reason Democrats salivate at the thought of increasing the percent of Hispanic voters from 10 percent of the electorate to 20 or 30 percent. With a pro-Democrat voting bloc of that magnitude, Democrats would be unbeatable at the voting booth.

So, the purpose of immigration reform is to make as many Hispanics eligible to vote as possible. It does not matter whether they are American born or foreign born, and it does not matter whether they are here legally or illegally. In other words, Democrats are working to stack the deck against conservatives and cancel out the vote of Tea Party members and all like-minded individuals! Non-Hispanics who complain about this massive form of voter manipulation are labeled racist or xenophobic, when it is the Democrats who are clearly engaging in racist behavior against non-Hispanics voters.

This, my fellow patriots, is why the leaders of both major political parties deceptively refer to our nation as a democracy and not a republic. As a republic, our rights are secured by the Constitution, but under mob rule in a democracy, our rights can be trampled by a manu-factured majority vote! And, they have been stacking that vote against us since at least the 1980s.

Just look at the recent history of California. In the 1960s Christian conservative Ronald Reagan was elected Governor of the Golden state. As a result of massive, uncontrolled immigration by Hispanics and others, Ronald Reagan would not be elected dog catcher in that state today! When compared to the 1980s, the economy of California is now in serious decline as immigrants overpopulate schoolrooms, hospital emer-gency rooms, and other public service organizations that are forced by corrupt politicians to accommodate illegal aliens who have violated our immigration laws. A review of 22 radio stations in California found that 10 were now Hispanic stations.

Most disturbing is the fact that the sinister tactic used to fundamentally transform the electorate of California is being used as a model for the other states. Nowhere is this more evident than in the state of Texas. The fundamental transformation of Texas will be achieved through immigration and reproduction. In November of 2010 the *DallasNews.com* reported that, across Texas, the 1.5 million illegal immigrants give birth to 60,000 babies each and every year. Because all of these babies receive automatic citizenship, they all become future voters. It was further noted that 74 percent of the babies born at Parkland Memorial Hospital in Texas came from the wombs of women who were noncitizens – and taxpayers are paying for the hospital care of both mothers and babies! Professor Jose Angel Gutierrez of Texas, who advocates the return of the American southwest to Mexico, has said, "We have an aging white America. They are not making babies. They are dying. It's a matter of time. The explosion is in our population."

Now, knowing that the vast majority of Hispanics will consistently vote for Democrats over Republicans, how do we explain efforts by John Boehner, John McCain, and other Republican leaders to join with Democrats in passing so-called immigration reform with a direct or indirect path toward citizenship? Once again, we find more evidence that there is one political party masquerading as two parties. While about 7 out of 10 Americans want secure borders before immigration reform is considered, the leadership of both parties are working together to defy the wishes of the American people! Instead of representing us, it is "them against us" on the issue of immigration.

As Michael Savage has often said, nations are defined by their borders, language, and culture. Our borders are routinely violated; we are told to press one for English and two for Spanish; and our culture is being replaced with so-called "multiculturalism." In other words, our borders, language, and culture are all under attack. Thus, our nation is under attack.

We know the Republican leadership represents the immediate problem. We also know the Tea Party is both the immediate and long-term solution. While the Republican leadership is aiding and abetting Democrats in destroying our borders, language, and culture, the Tea Party represents America's protective, traditional middle class. They are the guardians of our borders, language, and culture! Unrestrained immigration high-lights issues such as crime, jobs, welfare, health care, and budgets. But we also know that, in the long-term, the most critical issue is that of deliberate, sinister, demographic-based voter manipulation.

Simple Solutions!

Firstly, E-verify must be required for employment throughout this nation. If any public or private sector employer is caught knowingly hiring illegal immigrants, they must be prosecuted.

Secondly, it must be unlawful to rent or sell property to people who do not successfully pass through the E-verify system. Although E-verify has Big Brother implications, it is an effective solution to a sovereignty-destroying problem. If illegal immigrants cannot find a place to work nor a place to live, that population will eventually evaporate!

Thirdly, illegal presence in the United States should be changed from a civil offense to a criminal offense. Entering this country or remaining in this country illegally must be made a felony! This may sound harsh to some, but if this problem is not solved now, our grandchildren will never know what it was like to live in a free America!

Chapter Seven

The Media!

What Is The Role Of Newspapers,

Magazines, Radio, And The Internet?

What is the role of radio today, specifically talk radio? Back in the 1990s when Bill Clinton was president, talk radio was the primary tool that I used to convey the truth to the American people. This may be difficult to believe today, but talk radio was so new at that time the Clinton Administration initially paid little attention to it. As talk radio began to grow, I was able to secure interviews on many radio talk shows. Through this medium I was able to sidestep the liberal TV media and print media and get my message to the American people.

Today we are told that the largest audiences in talk radio are conservative. This is true. Liberals have not been as successful as conservatives in this arena. However, although the conservative audience is large, it is not as vast as some imagine it to be. When you study the audiences of Rush Limbaugh, Sean Hannity, and others, you find they have many of the same listeners. And, these are also the same people who watch Sean Hannity and other conservatives on the *Fox News Channel*. So, although conservative talk radio and cable television are important sources of news and information, their audiences tend to overlap. Therefore, they are oftentimes just preaching to the choir. I like to call this overlapping group of conservatives audience members "politicos."

Rush Limbaugh, the "king" of talk radio, is said to have about 14 million weekly listeners, and Sean Hannity is close at his heels with 13.5 million weekly listeners. However, the number of daily listeners is unknown, and is certainly much less than the number of weekly listeners. It must also be noted that these two conservative radio talk shows are counter-balanced by two leftist *NPR* radio programs with audience sizes that rival those of Limbaugh and Hannity. *NPR's Morning Edition* is a leftist public radio news program with 12.3 million weekly listeners, and *NPR's All Things Considered* is a leftist public radio news and talk show with 11.8 million weekly listeners.

Armed with this information, we must not have an inflated impression of the magnitude of the influence of conservative talk radio and cable television. Many conservatives were surprised by the election and re-election of a seriously flawed candidate like Barack Obama. Nearly every Obama weakness was exposed by conservative radio talk shows hosts, so, we believed he should never have seen the inside of the Oval Office. We were surprised by the election results because we falsely believed a sufficient number of voters must have been converted by Rush Limbaugh and others. They weren't! So, conservative talk radio is a necessary tool for success, but alone it is not sufficient!

Let's take a look at newspapers. As you may know, many have experienced a sharp decline in readership in recent years. Some have gone out of business. This significant loss of readership can be blamed on many factors. Firstly, newspaper editors and writers have shifted so far to the left, they have fallen into disfavor with readers who want an unbiased report of current events. Secondly, more Americans rely on talk radio and cable television for their news and information. Thirdly, the Internet has truly revolutionized how people stay informed. It is rightfully called the "information super-highway," traveled daily by owners of desktops, as well as laptops, smartphones, and other mobile devices.

Of those newspapers that are still in business, especially local, small town newspapers, we may ask how they gather news and information from around the world. They certainly cannot afford to have inter-national correspondents placed around the globe. The answer is, they stay informed through a news feed, such as *AP*, or the *Associated Press*. They may also tap into *UPI*, or *United Press International*, as well as other sources. So, one can manipulate nearly all secondary news sources in the nation simply by controlling a few major news feeds such as *AP* and *UPI*.

However, today the Internet is to the media what talk radio was back in the 1990s. With the Internet one can bypass the leftist media and seek contrary views from a nearly unlimited number of sources. With talk radio and the Internet, the leftist media monopoly is truly over! However, conservatives tend to restrict themselves to conservative news sites, and liberals tend to limit themselves of leftist news sites. So conservatives and liberals will go to websites where they will hear what they want to be told, and read what they want to examine.

Unfortunately, not all websites, whether conservative or liberal, are legitimate sources of news and information! To add to this problem, we have recently learned of Obama's plan to turn control of the Internet over to the international community. This means the Internet will ultimately fall under the control of the United Nations! This subversive activity by Obama is a tactic designed to stifle the free speech of his political opponents, such as the Tea Party, while blaming the restrictions on foreigners! It is an ominous end run around the First Amendment to the U.S. Constitution – the very document he has sworn to protect and defend!

According to *Gallup*, as of July, 2013, most Americans, about 55 percent, said they got their news from television. About 21 percent relied on the Internet, and only 9 percent said they turned to newspapers, magazines, and other print media. A mere 6 percent stated that they got their news from radio!

While news junkies turn to cable news sources, far more people rely on network news sources. For example, four top cable news sources, *Fox News*, *MSNBC*, *CNN*, and *HLN*, together average about 3.4 million primetime viewers. However, *ABC*, *CBS*, and *NBC* collectively average about 22 million viewers for their nightly network newscasts. The number of people seeking news from local TV news sources is difficult to determine, but the audience size is believed to far exceed that of the network news sources. So, while more people are seeking news from alternative sources, network and local news outlets remain top resources for tens of millions of Americans.

It should be noted that, while many conservatives hope the *Fox News Channel* will help them advance the Tea Party agenda, this cable news source attracts an average of 1.8 million viewers during primetime. The 1.6 million viewers who collectively rely on the leftists at *MSNBC*, *CNN*, and *HLN* for primetime news nearly cancel out those who turn to the *Fox News Channel*. Add the 22 million viewers who get their news from the decidedly leftist *ABC*, *CBS*, and *NBC* nightly network news teams and you can see that the conservative message is routinely overwhelmed by liberal talking points on America's TV screens.

Far too many Americans continue to believe the "spin" they routinely receive from the leftists who control national network and local television news sources. Too many people believe that, if it has been printed, it must be fit to print. Spin, of course, is just a euphemism for "lie." Fortunately, the leftist grip on their audiences has loosened a bit as a result of the devastating effect of ObamaCare. Millions of Americans have been forced to change doctors, have lost their health care plans, saw their premiums skyrocket, had their weekly work hours cut below 30 hours, or lost their jobs entirely – all as a result of this freedom-crushing piece of legislation. Because these leftist news sources supported ObamaCare and continue to defend it, they, like Obama, are viewed with a more skeptical attitude by their nationwide and local audiences.

The Left is now paying for their endless lies about ObamaCare. We must learn from this observation. Given the large amount of disinformation available on the Internet and from other media outlets, Tea Party members and other conservatives must be careful to verify all news and information. We must always check with sources that have proven to be reliable over time. Failing to do this, even once, can result in a loss of confidence in Tea Party members as reliable sources of news and information. This can dramatically hurt our cause, just as the multitude of intentional lies told by the Obama Administration has significantly damaged their cause!

Chapter Eight

What Role Does God Have

In Our Government Today?

"The Constitution was never meant to prevent people from praying; its declared purpose was to protect their freedom to pray." – President Ronald Reagan

In 1962 the U.S. Supreme Court banned prayer in America's public schools. In 1963 the Court prohibited Bible reading or the praying of the Lord's Prayer. In 1980 the U.S. Supreme Court ruled that it was unconstitutional for the Ten Commandments to be posted in a public school classroom. In 1992 the Court ruled it was unconstitutional for the state to sponsor prayer at school promotional activities and graduation ceremonies. In 2000 the U.S. Supreme Court ruled that student-led, student-initiated prayer before a football game was unconstitutional. William Rehnquist, Antonin

Scalia, and Clarence Thomas, the three dissenting justices in the 2000 ruling, wrote that the majority opinion rendered by the other six justices "bristles with hostility to all things religious in public life."

Collectively, in the above five cases the U.S. Supreme Court ruled that prayer, Bibles, and the Ten Commandments must be banned from government schools because such cases represented violations of the constitutional principle of "separation of church and state." However, "separation of church and state" can be found nowhere in the U.S. Constitution. Instead, we find the following "Establishment Clause" in the First Amendment to the U.S. Constitution: "Congress shall make no law respecting an establishment of religion."

It is further stated that Congress shall make no law "prohibiting the free exercise thereof." Again, nowhere in the U.S. Constitution do we find the words "separation of church and state," nor do we find a principle upon which the fabrication of such a phrase could be justified. What is clearly stated is that the federal government may not establish a religion, and it may not prohibit Americans from freely engaging in religious activities – such as praying, Bible reading, or posting of the Ten Commandments.

If we cannot find "separation of church and state" in the U.S. Constitution, where can we find it? We simply need to read Article 52 of the 1977 Soviet Constitution which stated the following: "Citizens of the USSR are guaranteed freedom of conscience, that is, the right to profess or not to profess any religion, and to conduct religious worship or atheistic propaganda. Incitement of hostility or hatred on religious grounds is prohibited. In the USSR, the church is separated from the state, and the school from the church." Similar Articles were placed in previous Soviet Constitutions as well!

A careful reading of the Bill of Rights reveals that it places restrictions on the U.S. Government, but not on "We the People." In order to transplant the Soviet constitutional principle of "separation of church and state" and construe it in the U.S. Constitution, the "justices" on the U.S. Supreme Court had to ignore or distort both the wording of the U.S. Constitution and the founder's original intent. In each of the five decisions previously outlined, the U.S. Supreme Court violated the following clearly stated constitutional principle: Congress, and thus the federal government, shall not prohibit the free exercise of religion – anywhere at any time. No exceptions are listed.

In addition, the First Amendment further states that the federal government may pass no law "abridging the freedom of speech." Clearly, voluntary, spoken prayer, as traditionally said at school graduations, football games, and in public school classrooms, would most certainly be deemed the type of "free speech" which the federal government may not abridge.

In establishing the doctrine of "separation of church and state" the U.S. Supreme Court made reference to a letter written by Thomas Jefferson in 1802. In this letter, written to the Danbury Baptist Association in Danbury, Connecticut, Jefferson addressed fears expressed by religious leaders that the First Amendment could be construed as granting freedom of religion, rather than acknowledging that it was a God-given, inalienable right. And if freedom of religion was government-given, then government could regulate religion. Jefferson sought to alleviate their fears by stating that religion was free from federal interference because the First Amendment provided "a wall of separation of Church and State." Clearly, Jefferson's "wall" protected the church from the state, not the state from the church. The First Amendment, as all other Amendments in the Bill of Rights, places restrictions on the federal government, not on the American people.

It must also be noted that, in his 1982 book, *The Second American Revolution*, John W. Whitehead reported that Thomas Jefferson not only founded the University of Virginia, but he also encouraged students to meet, pray, and worship together on campus. Jefferson further encouraged students to meet and pray on campus with their professors. Whitehead also noted that Jefferson authored the first plan of public education, which was adopted by the City of Washington. In this public educational plan Thomas Jefferson recommended the employment of the Bible and the Isaac Watts Hymnal as teaching aides to help students learn how to read.

As reported by WND.com, Congressman Louie Gohmert, a Republican from Texas, said that our forefathers saw the U.S. Constitution as a document designed to protect the church from the state, and not vice versa. Gohmert said, for example, that James Madison, who is recognized as the father of the U.S. Constitution, attended non-denominational Christian worship services every Sunday inside the U.S. Capitol, which is now called Statuary Hall. James Madison was joined by Thomas Jefferson, the primary author of the Declaration of Independence. So, two Founding Fathers, both of whom served as presidents of the United States, met to pray and worship God every Sunday on government property. Yes, they prayed inside the very chamber where Congress routinely conducted government business from 1807 to 1857.

In light of Jefferson's encouragement of students to pray on the public University of Virginia campus – even with their professors, and his educational plan that included the use of the Bible (which contains the Ten Commandments) to teach reading in public schools, and the fact Thomas Jefferson attended Christian church services on federal government property, how could any honest, rational person conclude that Thomas Jefferson believed in a "wall of separation" that prohibited prayer, Bible reading, and the posting of the Ten Commandments in American public schools or on any government property? How could anyone conclude that the federal government could prohibit the free exercise of religion in this manner when the U.S. Constitution states, in plain English, that the federal government may not prohibit the free exercise of religion? How could anyone conclude that a taxpayer could not pray on taxpayer-funded property?

It should be noted that the last paragraph of the U.S. Constitution states the following: "Done in convention, by the unanimous consent of the states present, the 17th day of September, **in the year of our Lord 1787**, and of the independence of the United States of America the 12th. In Witness thereof we have hereunto subscribed our names." (Bold lettering added)

Such wording, "**in the year of our Lord 1787**," clearly violates the constitutional principle of "separation of church and state" as defined by the federal government today! Therefore, according to the U.S. Supreme Court, the U.S. Constitution is unconstitutional! The fact that the U.S. Constitution contains the words "**in the year of our Lord 1787**" demonstrates beyond all doubt that Court decisions regarding "separation of church and state" were, and remain, conspicuously illogical and therefore indefensible!

Because news, information, and education are dominated by the political Left, most Americans are truly ignorant of the role of God and religion in the lives of our Founding Fathers. Most Americans do not know the founders of our government were deeply committed to their religious faith and the concept of religious liberty.

Does The World Love Your Pastor?

At the core of the Tea Party we find Bible-based conservative Christians. They are moral people who wish to see a return to honest, lawful, constitutional government. However, this will never happen unless we restore God to his rightful place – at the center of our government and our society! When the U.S. Supreme Court began to remove God from the public sector of our culture in 1962, we have seen a continuous growth in government and a steady decline in our personal freedom.

In *Deuteronomy 8:19-20*, we find that God has destroyed nations which have turned their backs against Him, and He warns us that we also risk destruction if we follow the same path. Therefore, we must return God to government, but we can only do so through the efforts of Godly people. Tea Party members and other Bible-believing conservative Christians must work together to achieve this goal. We must approach our pastors and ask them to publicly address this issue.

When pastors are approached, they often state that they do not want to mix politics with religion, and therefore decline to speak to their congregations about the need to return God to government. But we must remind them of *Ephesians 6:12*, where we find the following: "For we wrestle not against flesh and blood, but against principalities, against powers, against the rulers of the darkness of this world, against spiritual wickedness in high places." So, the Bible tells us that when we challenge corrupt flesh and blood politicians, bureaucrats, and their minions, we are not fighting against them, but against the dark spiritual forces operating behind them. And it is most certainly the duty of every Christian to battle "against spiritual wickedness in high places." Ask your pastor if he recognizes this as his solemn duty.

Your pastor may complain that his church is registered with the government as a 501(c)(3). Therefore, he will jeopardize his tax exempt status if he engages in political activities. However, the IRS website states that a tax exempt 501(c)(3) organization "may not attempt to influence legislation as a substantial part of its activities and it may not participate in any campaign activity for or against political candidates."

At the chalcedon.edu website your pastor can be guided by former IRS agents and tax attorneys. They will inform your pastor that all churches automatically have tax exempt status with the IRS whether or not they have 501(c)(3) status. Secondly, your pastor will learn that he can endlessly engage in issue advocacy. Such speech by your pastor is protected by the First Amendment to the U.S. Constitution. According to a pamphlet issued by the *Alliance Defense Fund*, "Issue advocacy, however, may not be limited by government and can be freely engaged in by churches. As long as one does not use explicit words expressly advocating the election or defeat of a clearly identified candidate, one is free to praise or criticize officials and candidates – this is called issue advocacy." Also, according to the *Alliance Defense Fund* (name changed to *Alliance Defending Freedom*), there is no law that restricts churches from defining moral positions and asking people to vote accordingly.

So, after educating your pastor, if necessary, hand him a signed petition requesting that he address his congregation with the need to return God to government. Perhaps the petition could include the two Bible messages from *Deuteronomy* and *Ephesians* as we have just noted. Have the petition signed by as many like-minded individuals as possible from among the pastor's flock. The more signatures you garner the more persuasive will be your petition. Your pastor will know that for every single signature on the petition, there may be 10, 20, or more members of his flock who are also concerned about the disastrous course this nation has been following since at least the 1960s. Pastors always take a head count, for they know the larger the number of sheep in their fold, the larger will be the collection offering.

Remind him that pastors played a leading role in the American Revolution, and perhaps God has put him in his current position so he can lead his people in a revival to restore the Godly nation founded by our forefathers. Remind your pastor that, like the pastors before him, he must be guided by *2 Corinthians 3:17*: "Now the Lord is that Spirit; and where the Spirit of the Lord is, there is liberty." Conversely, when the Spirit of the Lord is absent, there is bondage, and we have been sliding into increasing levels of bondage for many generations. It's time to reverse course! It's time for your pastor to lead a revival!

Remind your pastor that he is not here to be liked, but to save souls! Providing him with the following verses from *Matthew 10:22*, which contain the words of Jesus, may be helpful: "And ye shall be hated of all men for my name's sake; but he that endureth to the end shall be saved." You could also add these two versus from *John 15:18-19*: "If the world hate you, ye know that it hated me before it hated you. If ye were of this world, the world would love his own: but because ye are not of the world, but I have chosen you out of the world, therefore the world hateth you." Ask you pastor, does the world hate him the way it hated Jesus? If he wants to be loved by the world, he is certainly not following in the footsteps of Jesus!

If your pastor decides he would rather be loved by the world and refuses to help us put God back into government, it may be time for you to seek a new pastor and a new church! You may also remind him that the Bible addresses sins of omission as well as sins of commission. Clearly, if your pastor is not part of the solution, then he is, by default, part of the problem! Whether or not you receive the help of your pastor, you must keep fighting the fight! You must continue to join forces with like-minded citizens and work to return America to its founding principles.

Finally, ask your pastor what he is doing to stop the spread of Islam in our schools and our government? Among Muslims there is no such thing as "separation of church and state." An Islamic state is a theocracy, and infidels must either convert to Islam or be beheaded. Those who get their news and information outside the so-called mainstream media know that Islam has infiltrated our public schools, as well as our government. A simple Internet search will reveal many examples. But now we must ask, why has Christianity been expelled from our schools and replaced with Islam? Why does the Soviet constitutional principle of "separation of church and state" apply to Christianity but not to Islam? What hypocrisy!

Tea Party members make up a small, but determined group of American patriots. They must expand their numbers. By enlisting the help of preachers and pastors nationwide the Tea Party can tap into thousands of churches which contain millions of like-minded individuals. Many conservative Christian Americans are busy making a living and raising a family, and politics is often placed on the back burner. But time is short. It's time to get them involved in politics. As a matter of fact, it may be now or never!

As noted in Chapter Six regarding immigration, the number of liberal and left-leaning moderate voters will increase dramatically as immigration increases, and especially in the event amnesty is granted. Tea Party voters and like-minded voters may soon be over-whelmed at the polls. As stated in Chapter Four, that is why we hear false claims that we are a democracy, which is essentially mob rule. We may simply be outnumbered by foreign-born voters who do not share our traditional American values of limited, lawful, constitutional government. And, as reported earlier in Chapter Six, this is the true purpose of unchecked immigration. It's not about jobs, but about cancelling out your vote and the votes of other conservative Christians! Yes, time is short, but if necessary re-read Chapters Four and Six to refresh your memory!

Although estimates vary, many believe there are about 330,000 Christian churches in America today. In January, 2014 *Gallup* reported that 38 percent of Americans self-identify as conservative, 23 percent as liberal, and 39 percent as moderate. If the political orientation of Christian churches are consistent with these percentages, conservative and moderate pastors and their congregations make up 77 percent of church attendees. Thus, of the 330,000 Christian churches in America, perhaps as many as 77 percent, or 254,100, may be receptive to the Tea Party message! This is the gold mine we Christian conservatives must tap into.

Chapter Nine

The Righteous

Are As Bold As A Lion!

Proverbs 28: 1

"We must now face the harsh truth that the objectives of communism are being steadily advanced because many of us do not recognize the means used to advance them...The individual is handicapped by coming face to face with a Conspiracy so monstrous he cannot believe it exists. The American mind simply has not come to a realization of the evil which has been introduced into our midst." – J. Edgar Hoover, FBI Director, *Elks Magazine*, August, 1956

The above quote, like most of the material in this chapter, has been excerpted from the book, *Welcome to Soviet America: Special Edition*. Although the above quote by J. Edgar Hoover was written around 60 years ago, it is just as relevant today as it was in 1956. Both then, and now, "The American mind simply has not come to a realization of the evil which has been introduced into our midst." This chapter was written to encourage the reader to do precisely that. We must all acknowledge that evil exists, and that it has been corrupting the very fabric of our society for many generations. We must acknowledge this publicly as well as privately, just as other bold Americans have done!

Political correctness, which is just another label for cultural Marxism, must no longer prohibit us from boldly telling the truth. In *Proverbs 28:1*, we are told the following: "The wicked flee when no man pursueth; but the righteous are as bold as a lion." For far too long we have been timid when we should have been bold. For this reason Jeff Snyder titled his book, *Nation of Cowards*, and Judge Andrew P. Napolitano titled one of his books as follows: *A Nation of Sheep*.

Judge Napolitano describes how we the people are being led down a very dangerous path where the federal government bypasses the U.S. Constitution to rob us of our rights and freedoms. He warns us that too many Americans are standing silent as the federal government systematically destroys the very freedoms it was designed to protect. Judge Napolitano asks, are you a sheep or a wolf? Are you a sheep that will stand by silently as your freedom and dignity as a human being are destroyed, or, are you a wolf that will fight for your God-given rights? Clearly, "We the People" must become as wolves. We must now be as bold as a lion, as instructed in the Bible. If we do not fight for our rights now, they will soon be lost forever!

Welcome To Soviet America!

In 1932 William Z. Foster, the National Chairman of the Community Party, USA, wrote a book titled *Toward Soviet America.* In his book Foster described many Communist goals and objectives that would be pursued to realize the Communist dream of constructing a Soviet America. Few Americans took Foster seriously. Few Americans took the warnings of J. Edgar Hoover seriously. Those who did so were ridiculed. Their ridicule was compounded with extreme frustration as they watched one published Communist goal after another being achieved while the bulk of the American people lived in blissful ignorance and denial. Most

Americans simply could not believe the Sovereign America founded by George Washington, Thomas Jefferson, and James Madison could ever be subverted and transformed into an American version of the now defunct Soviet Union. Surely a self-governing America could never resemble the Soviet slave state operated by genocidal maniacs like Vladimir Lenin, Joseph Stalin, and Nikita Khrushchev!

But increasing numbers of knowledgeable Americans today are asserting unequivocally that the evidence of an encroaching Soviet America can no longer be denied. Conservatives who once laughed at those who warned of an impending Soviet America are no longer laughing. Many have been left stunned and bewildered. Some report a sense of unreality regarding the events that are unfolding before their very eyes on a daily basis. Only now, nearly six decades later, are they beginning to understand what J. Edgar Hoover meant when he said the American mind has been presented with a criminal conspiracy that is so monstrous, so evil, that we cannot believe it actually exists; we cannot believe that this evil is within our midst and accomplishing one diabolical goal after another, decade after decade – right in front of our eyes!

The evidence for the existence of the "evil" that J. Edgar Hoover spoke of nearly 60 years ago is overwhelming, and many prominent individuals are publicly speaking out – as boldly as a lion! Let's review some documented quotes from a wide variety of astute observers of the human condition who have concluded that William Z. Foster's dream of a Soviet America is, indeed, becoming a reality – and FBI Director J. Edgar Hoover's assessment was undoubtedly accurate.

Gerald Celente, the Founder and Director of *The Trends Research Institute*, spoke to George Noory in 2008 on the late-night radio program *Coast to Coast AM*. After observing intrusive, heavy-handed federal involvement in the private U.S. banking system and the private financial affairs of the American people, Gerald Celente proclaimed that, "This is becoming the USSA – the United States of Soviet America!" Clearly, Gerald Celente was describing a fundamental characteristic of the "Soviet America" predicted by Communist William Z. Foster in 1932. In a return appearance five months later Gerald Celente transposed a few words and stated that, "We're becoming the USSA - the United Soviet States of America." Seventy-six years earlier William Z. Foster predicted that Americans would one day live in

"The United Soviet States of America," and he used those very words to title the last chapter of his book.

When Rush Limbaugh was discussing Obama's plans for America with Sean Hannity, Rush said, "I don't know where – what he [Obama] wants to try has worked. It didn't work in the Soviet Union." In addition, Rush reported that liberal Democrats were using the power of the federal government to intimidate him. They were trying to silence him by distorting his words, publicly denouncing him, and sending a critical letter to the management of Premiere Radio Networks. Rush characterized such behavior as follows: "...I think they've become Stalinist-like...this is not just liberalism. It's Stalinist, using the power of the state to intimidate citizens." Rush made a transcript of this program available to his listeners, and titled the transcript *"Stalinists Have Taken Over the Left."* (Underline added)

In 1960 Billy James Hargis wrote a book titled, *Communist America... Must It Be?* In his book Hargis warned that powerful forces were at work to create a Communist America. Nearly fifty years later we find concerned Americans, such as Glenn Beck, making the following alarming statements: "We are now more

Communist than China," and, "...both sides [Democrats and Republicans] are running towards bigger government. We're practically the Soviet Union." Billy James Hargis further wrote that, "The American people need to see communism for what it really is, whether disguised as liberalism, socialism, progressivism, or modernism." Nearly fifty years later Michael Savage would state that, "It's chilling to see how much we've become like the ex-Soviet Union – thanks to liberalism!" (Underlines added for emphasis.)

So, more and more prominent Americans are beginning to wake up. Finally, they are now facing "the harsh truth that the objectives of communism are being steadily advanced" in this nation, and they are coming "to a realization of the evil which has been introduced into our midst," just as J. Edgar warned us about in 1956.

You Are The Solution!

Tea Party members and other conservative Christians must now follow the examples given in the previous paragraphs. We must call liberalism and progressivism for what they are; today they are simply euphemisms for communism.

We know that leftists boldly tell huge, bald-faced lies. And they tell them over and over again until millions of Americans actually believe those lies. From the global warming/climate change hoax which has been per-petrated upon the entire global community, to the lie of "separation of church and state," to the lies behind abortion, gun control, and socialized medicine, they never stop! They lie openly, boldly, confidently, and they demand that honest people believe, or at least pretend to believe, each and every lie!

If they can successfully sell their lies, why can't we successfully sell the truth? We must not be afraid to use the words Marxist, Leninist, Stalinist, Communist, and fascist, when describing the Left. We may ask, why is the Left winning the so-called same sex or gay marriage debate? They are winning simply because too many prominent conservative Christians are too timid to boldly tell the truth. We must be as bold as a lion, as stated in the Bible.

We must boldly state in public that we oppose same sex marriage or gay marriage for two obvious reasons: Firstly, the Bible tells us that homosexual behavior is sinful. Therefore, a Christian cannot support that which is condemned as sinful in the Bible. Secondly, from among the 45 Communist goals found in the 1962 book, *The Naked Communist*, we find that Communist goal number 26 is as follows: "Present homo-sexuality, degeneracy and promiscuity as normal, natural, healthy." It should be noted that this Communist goal, along with the other 44 Communist goals, were entered into the *Congressional Record* in 1963 by Representative Albert Herlong, Jr., a conservative Democrat from Florida. The reader may review these 45 Communist goals at the website, WelcomeToSovietAmerica.Net.

Is Jeff Snyder correct? Are we a "Nation of Cowards," to fearful to simply tell the truth? Are we too sheepish to fight for rights and liberties that are clearly delineated in the U.S. Constitution, as Judge Andrew P. Napolitano has suggested? If we are too fearful to call a Communist goal a Communist goal when it has been documented as such and entered into the *Congressional Record*, then we are no longer living in America. Then we are clearly living in a Soviet-style America where people are afraid to speak the truth.

"The hottest places in hell are reserved for those who, in a period of moral crisis, maintain their neutrality." – Alighieri Dante

Chapter Ten

The Role Each American Must Play

If We Are To Win Back Our Freedom!

Victory In Pennsylvania!

A small number of people tend to vote in primary elections as well as special elections at the local level; therefore, a highly motivated, well-organized effort at the grassroots level can achieve amazing results. But don't take my word for it, just look at a recent election in Pennsylvania!

On March 20, 2014, Spectator.org reported a story with the following eye-opening headline: "Scott Wagner Beats the GOP Establishment!" Scott Wagner is a conservative Republican businessman. He was backed by a grassroots conservative organization called *Citizens Alliance of Pennsylvania*, or *CAP*. This organization is not affiliated with the Tea Party, and was actually formed several years before the Tea Party movement.

Although establishment Republicans changed the rules so Scott Wagner's name would not be on the ballot, and they spent $350,000 to defeat him, this conservative Republican was able to achieve victory. Although Scott Wagner was a write-in candidate, he won an astounding 48 percent of the vote in a three-way race. The establishment Republican received 27 percent, and the Democrat garnered 26 percent of the vote. Conservative Republican Scott Wagner, with the support of *Citizens Alliance of Pennsylvania*, literally made political history.

What is the lesson here for the Tea Party and like-minded conservatives? The lesson is simply this: Establishment Republicans and Democrats can be soundly defeated by a grassroots effort when voters are highly motivated. The Left knows that an emotionally charged voting public is the key to victory. That's why they inflame women with phony reports of sexism, enrage blacks and Hispanics with false claims of racism, and infuriate gays with pseudo reports of homo-phobia, etc. Unlike the Left, we must arm voters with facts, not lies, and anger, not hatred. The key to victory for conservative Christians is the generation of a fact-based, "righteous anger" among the voting public.

While conservatives have been successful in electing some Tea Party backed politicians at the federal level, the federal system is so corrupt that it is nearly impossible to change it from within. For this reason we must focus on local elections. We must concentrate on state legislatures. If we can fill state chambers with Constitution defending conservatives, we can fundamentally transform Washington D.C. from the outside.

Recently Congressman Mike Rogers, a Republican from Michigan, stated that he will not run for re-election. Rogers stated that he can be more effective in changing the federal government from the outside as a radio talk show host rather than working inside as a Congressman. This is an astounding statement from a U.S. Representative who holds the powerful position of Chairman of the Permanent Select Committee on Intelligence. Just stop and think about that for a few moments!

Also, we must remind our family, friends, and neighbors of the horrors of ObamaCare. Commit to memory the fact that, under ObamaCare, millions of Americans have lost their health care plans. These people paid for their plans either directly as individuals, or indirectly through their employers. And, millions of people who chose not to pay for a health care plan are now having their plan paid for by those who lost their original health care plans! What a disaster! Remind everyone that millions of Americans lost their health care plans after Obama boldly stated about three dozen times that no one would lose their plans as a result of ObamaCare. This repeated falsehood has justly been called the "Lie of the year!"

Your Assignment:

Victory In Your Home State!

Forget what you know about politics. Don't run against candidates, run against the enemies of a free election. Run against Steve LaTourette, Karl Rove, and the RNC hierarchy. All three are political enemies of conservatives. They are raising millions of dollars for the sole purpose of destroying the Tea Party. Republican Steve LaTourette, for example, is being financed by labor unions. As you may know, labor unions are a core constituency of the Democratic Party. Therefore, Steve LaTourette certainly has the appearance of a Democrat mole operating subversively within the Republican Party! No Republican should support this traitor! Also, it has been reported that the *U.S. Chamber of Commerce* has pledged $50 million to establishment Republicans in order to crush the Tea Party and elect "centrist Republicans" in primary elections. Obviously, your most dangerous political enemies are those who are raising millions of dollars to destroy the Tea Party.

Don't worry about incumbents. We cannot outspend them. But we can send out millions of tweets, Facebook messages, and emails. And every message must be the same: Establishment Republicans are working to rob Tea Party backed candidates of free and fair elections. They are working to crush the Tea Party and the spirit that energizes the Tea Party. They want us to submit! Repeat this message over and over again, and do not make the mistake of assuming that all voters know that establishment Republicans are working to destroy us!

Every Tea Party member must help spread the messages found in this handbook. We must tell our fellow conservative Christians that establishment Republicans have declared open warfare against us, and we have no choice but to fight back. They can spend millions of dollars, but they cannot buy your vote if you are not willing to sell it. So, let them spend millions of dollars that will have little effect. Because the Tea Party is made up of many diverse groups, they will have much difficulty fooling us and stopping our movement.

If we follow the plan in this handbook, we can beat establishment Republicans just as our fellow conservatives did in Pennsylvania. Victory has been achieved, and the time is ripe to do it over and over again. We must make our social network our information super-highway. We must encourage others to spread the word and inform like-minded Americans that the *U.S. Chamber of Commerce* has pledged up to $50 million to those who are working to destroy us. Through our social network we must motivate others to attack this problem at its source. Stated simply, we must cut off their money supply.

How do we do that? In our hometowns and neighborhoods we, and those in our social network, must visit our local *Chamber of Commerce* and express our personal dissatisfaction with their leadership at the national level. If they are unaware, we must tell them of the millions of dollars their national leadership has committed to the destruction of the Tea Party. Squads of Tea Party members must visit local businesses around the nation that publicly display their member-ship in the *Chamber of Commerce*. Inform the managers of those businesses that you, your family, and your friends will no longer shop at any business that is a member of the *Chamber of Commerce*.

If we can get local businesses to call the national *Chamber* and complain, we can have a huge impact. Keep in mind that many businesses belong to a local *Chamber* simply as a matter of tradition. If many fear a loss of customers, they may leave this anti-Tea Party organization. This must be done at the local, state, and national level. Do not underestimate the power of this action. If a small but powerful group of gays can force a CEO from office, a small but dedicated group of conservatives can achieve equally amazing results.

Brendan Eich, the CEO of *Mozilla*, the company which operates the web browser Firefox, was forced out of office in April of 2014. What was his crime? He donated $1,000 to back Proposition 8, which defined marriage as a union between a man and a woman in the state of California. By forcing a CEO out of office, a small group of gays got big results, and so can we! Remember, the Tea Party is an army! As dedicated warriors we must challenge and defeat our political enemies at every turn. When they bring money, we bring people. When they boycott, we have a bigger boycott. We are in a war, and we must fight on every front.

The weakness in both major parties is turnout. In most counties and states we can outnumber the opposition if we increase our turnout. We must go to the churches and talk to the pastors. Churches are a great political asset in general elections. However, we don't have large numbers, so we need the churches to augment the Tea Party vote in primary elections as well. We must motivate the pastors. They must not get involved in campaigning. That's the job of the candidates. The job of the pastors is to put God back into government and stop the spread of Islam – without getting involved in politics.

Ten Steps To Victory At The Polls!

If every Tea Party member follows these ten simple steps, victory at the polls is guaranteed!

One: Make a list of all members in your Tea Party group.

Two: Make a list of all the people you know in other Tea Party groups.

Three: As soon as possible, spread the word about this handbook to all members of your Tea Party group and other Tea Party groups.

Four: As your personal tool to fight this battle, make daily use the social media network, such as twitter, Facebook, and emails, and spread the messages in this handbook.

Five: Every Tea Party member needs to pick a favorite message from this handbook, and bring it up in casual conversations. For example, if the message in Chapter Four appeals to you, talk to your friends, relatives, neighbors, and co-workers about the fact that today, the Pledge of Allegiance has become a lie! Or, talk to them about Chapter Six, and let them know immigration is not about jobs, but about cancelling out their vote!

Six: Get several copies of this handbook and circulate them among like-minded people. (Yes, this may sound self-serving, but it is necessary)

Seven: Make a sample ballot, and in simple language, tell prospective voters who to vote for.

Eight: Make a list of 10 people, and recruit them to go to the polls on Election Day. If necessary, help arrange transportation. Give each person a copy of your sample ballot. As an added benefit, this process can help to expose voter fraud. If your combined lists indicate, for example, that 200 people voted for a Tea Party-backed candidate in your district, and the election results show that only 100 did so, we have caught them red-handed!

Nine: Go to nursing homes, private homes, and apartments in your community and talk with your elderly neighbors. Let them use your sample ballot as a guide, and help them fill out their absentee ballots. Offer to mail their absentee ballots for them.

Ten: Hold meetings in your home and discuss the contents of this handbook. When everyone becomes well-informed, have each person in your home group hold meetings in their own homes.

A Final Note!

This may seem challenging to you, but consider what is at stake. We are literally fighting for political survival, and time is very short. Also, think of the American soldier in Afghanistan, who is fighting not for his political survival, but for his personal survival. He is most certainly afraid, but he will do his duty, even if it costs him his life. The challenges we face pale in comparison to the challenges he faces! Now, each of us must do our duty! No excuses!

In closing, if every person who reads this handbook follows these ten steps exactly, we will win. At the first printing of this handbook (April, 2014), we find that a Republican primary is just a few weeks away in many states. So, move swiftly. The eBook version of this handbook (available at Lulu.com) places important tools in the hands of voters immediately. By design, this handbook can be read in just one or two hours. This was done so that people can take this information and digest it without being overwhelmed with details.

As the author, it was not my mission to impress you with my ability to write a book, but to give you an effective tool to lead us to victory. So, once again, join with me and spread the information in this handbook with others at the speed of the social media networks. Time is critical. If you are truly a Tea Party warrior, fight for the ideals you so strongly believe. If you are a moral conservative Christian soldier, fight to preserve our nation in the image of God as it was intended by our Founding Fathers. From the author: **Fight**!

A Special Message!

From Pastor Ernie Sanders

President Of The

Geauga County Tea Party In Ohio

For those seeking guidance and inspiration during these challenging times, the following Bible verses have been assembled for your review. The reader will find that these biblical words are just as relevant today as the day they were first written. Some of these words may have been written precisely for those of us who are now confronting what J. Edgar Hoover described as "the evil which has been introduced into our midst."

We Must Be Doers Of The Word!

It is recommended that you start with *Matthew Chapter 7, verses 21 through 25*. In these verses we find that we must be "doers of the word," that is, we must be doers of the word of God as found in the Bible, and not just readers of the word. Also, we must not be doers of iniquity. If we become "doers of the word," we will be as wise men who built their houses upon a rock, and the rains, floods, and winds will not destroy them. Therefore, to be as solid as a rock in the eyes of God, we must be doers of His word as found in the Bible.

"Not everyone who says to me, Lord, Lord, will enter the kingdom of heaven, but only the one who does the will of my Father in heaven. Many will say to me in that day, Lord, Lord, have we not prophesied in thy name? and in thy name have cast out devils? and in thy name done many wonderful works? And then will I profess unto them, I never knew you: depart from me, ye that work iniquity. Therefore whosoever heareth these sayings of mine, and doeth them, I will liken him unto a wise man, which built his house upon a rock: And the rain descended, and the floods came, and the winds blew, and beat upon that house; and it fell not: for it was founded upon a rock." – *Matthew 7:21-25*

Yes, our God is an awesome God. Without exception, He has always done what He said He would do. And He does it exactly how, where, when and why He said He would do it!

In *Matthew Chapter 24 verse 35* we find the following: "Heaven and earth shall pass away, but my words shall not pass away." There is no other credible explanation of past, present, and future. The word "history," in reality, is a reference to His story, meaning God's word. He created the universe and all that is contained within. God's creation, which unfolds in front of us each day, is truly miraculous. But even greater than this miracle is the miracle of salvation of the lost and their reward of eternal life!

"In the beginning was the Word, and the Word was with God, and the Word was God. The same was in the beginning with God. All things were made by him; and without him was not any thing made that was made. In him was life; and the life was the light of men. And the light shineth in darkness; and the darkness com-prehended it not. There was a man sent from God, whose name *was* John. The same came for a witness, to bear witness of the Light, that all *men* through him might believe. He was not that Light, but *was sent* to bear witness of that Light. *That* was the true Light, which lighteth every man that cometh into the world. He was in the world, and the world was made by him, and the world knew him not. He came unto his own, and his own received him not. But as many as received him, to them gave he power to become the sons of God, *even* to them that believe on his name." – *John 1:1-12*

He Raised Up The Old Testament

Prophets For Their Day!

"And what shall I more say? for the time would fail me to tell of Gedeon, and *of* Barak, and *of* Samson, and *of* Jephthae; *of* David also, and Samuel, and *of* the prophets: Who through faith subdued kingdoms, wrought righteousness, obtained promises, stopped the mouths of lions, Quenched the violence of fire, escaped the edge of the sword, out of weakness were made strong, waxed valiant in fight, turned to flight the armies of the aliens. Women received their dead raised to life again: and others were tortured, not accepting deliverance; that they might obtain a better resurrection: And others had trial of *cruel* mockings and scourgings, yea, moreover of bonds and imprisonment: They were stoned, they were sawn asunder, were tempted, were slain with the sword: they wandered about in sheepskins and goatskins; being destitute, afflicted, tormented; (Of whom the world was not worthy:) they wandered in deserts, and *in* mountains, and *in* dens and caves of the earth. And these all, having obtained a good report through faith, received not the promise: God having provided some better thing for us, that they without us should not be made perfect." – *Hebrews 11:32-40*

He Raised Up New Testament

Christians For Their Day!

"And Jesus came and spake unto them, saying, All power is given unto me in heaven and in earth. Go ye therefore, and teach all nations, baptizing them in the name of the Father, and of the Son, and of the Holy Ghost: Teaching them to observe all things whatsoever I have commanded you: and, lo, I am with you always, *even* unto the end of the world. Amen." – *Matthew 28:18-20*

He Raised Up Our Nation's Founding Fathers Along With The Black Robed Regiment (Clergy) For Their Day. And Now He Is Calling Us.

Will You Answer The Call?

Or Will You Forever Wish You Had?

"According to the grace of God which is given unto me, as a wise masterbuilder, I have laid the foundation, and another buildeth thereon. But let every man take heed how he buildeth thereupon. For other foundation can no man lay than that is laid, which is Jesus Christ. Now if any man build upon this foundation gold, silver, precious stones, wood, hay, stubble; Every man's work shall be made manifest: for the day shall declare it, because it shall be revealed by fire; and the fire shall try every man's work of what sort it is. If any man's work abide which he hath built thereupon, he shall receive a reward. If any man's work shall be burned, he shall suffer loss: but he himself shall be saved; yet so as by fire. Know ye not that ye are the temple of God, and *that* the Spirit of God dwelleth in you?" – *1 Corinthians 3:10-16*

He Let Us Know There Would Be

A Price To Pay For Our Faith In Him!

"If the world hate you, ye know that it hated me before *it hated* you. If ye were of the world, the world would love his own: but because ye are not of the world, but I have chosen you out of the world, therefore the world hateth you. Remember the word that I said unto you, The servant is not greater than his lord. If they have persecuted me, they will also persecute you; if they have kept my saying, they will keep yours also. But all these things will they do unto you for my name's sake, because they know not him that sent me." – *John 15:18-21*

"But evil men and seducers shall wax worse and worse, deceiving, and being deceived. But continue thou in the things which thou hast learned and hast been assured of, knowing of whom thou hast learned *them*; And that from a child thou hast known the holy scriptures, which are able to make thee wise unto salvation through faith which is in Christ Jesus. All scripture *is* given by inspiration of God, and *is* profitable for doctrine, for reproof, for correction, for instruction in righteousness: That the man of God may be perfect, thoroughly furnished unto all good works." – *2 Timothy 3:13-17*

The Good News However, Is This:

The Suffering That We Experience

Is Hardly Worth Mentioning Compared To

The Rewards That We Will Receive!

"But watch thou in all things, endure afflictions, do the work of an evangelist, make full proof of thy ministry. For I am now ready to be offered, and the time of my departure is at hand. I have fought a good fight, I have finished *my* course, I have kept the faith: Henceforth there is laid up for me a crown of righteousness, which the Lord, the righteous judge, shall give me at that day: and not to me only, but unto all them also that love his appearing." – *2 Timothy 4:5-8*

"Let not your heart be troubled: ye believe in God, believe also in me. In my Father's house are many mansions: if *it were* not *so,* I would have told you. I go to prepare a place for you. And if I go and prepare a place for you, I will come again, and receive you unto myself; that where I am, *there* ye may be also. And whither I go ye know, and the way ye know." – *John 14:1-4*

"Nay, in all these things we are more than conquerors through him that loved us. For I am persuaded, that neither death, nor life, nor angels, nor principalities, nor powers, nor things present, nor things to come, Nor height, nor depth, nor any other creature, shall be able to separate us from the love of God, which is in Christ Jesus our Lord." – *Romans 8:37-39*

Well, I guess it just doesn't get any better than that!

Enough said!

Your brother in Christ Jesus,

Pastor Ernie Sanders

www.ingramcontent.com/pod-product-compliance
Lightning Source LLC
Chambersburg PA
CBHW060636290526
45793CB00001B/270